The Lord's Taverners
CRICKET
QUIZ BOOK

Compiled by Graham Tarrant

Foreword by Richie Benaud

David & Charles
Newton Abbot   London   North Pomfret (Vt)

PICTURE CREDITS

1a, 1c, 3a, 3b, 4a, 4b, 5a, 5b, 6a, 6b, 6c, 7a, 7b, 7c, 8a
(*Keystone Press Agency*)
2a, 2b, 8b (*Ken Kelly*)
1b (*by courtesy of Jim Laker*)

British Library Cataloguing in Publication Data

Tarrant, Graham
    The Lord's Taverners cricket quiz book.
    1. Cricket—Miscellanea
    I. Title
    796.35'8'076   GV917

   ISBN 0–7153–8633–6

Typeset by Northern Phototypesetting Co, Bolton
and printed in Great Britain
by Billings & Sons Ltd, Worcester
for David & Charles (Publishers) Limited
Brunel House Newton Abbot Devon

Published in the United States of America
by David & Charles Inc
North Pomfret Vermont 05053 USA

AUTHOR'S NOTE

A question is only easy if you know the answer, and hard if you don't; but in compiling the 600 or so questions that make up this book I have tried to take into account the different levels of interest in the game, and the fact that some people's cricketing memories are a lot longer than others.

Literally dozens of books have been used as reference sources, not all of them primarily cricket books and far too many to list here. However, I owe a special debt of thanks to Bill Frindall for his various works, among them *The Wisden Book of Test Cricket 1876–77 to 1977–78* and *The Guinness Book of Cricket Facts & Feats*; to Christopher Martin-Jenkins for *The Complete Who's Who of Test Cricketers*; to the *Wisden Cricketers' Almanack*, year after year; and to my friend Tony Mallerman for his ingeniously constructed anagrams.

G.T.

Foreword

There is no game more argued about, more controversial and more stimulating of healthy discussion than cricket. Nor is there any game where more comprehensive records and statistics are kept, statistics which provide the base for challenging questions about a five day stretch where players might battle with all their courage and skill and still not achieve a result.

The game, as is the case with life, is filled with heroes and failures, hard triers and some who never give enough, those who enjoy playing and others who look as though it would be difficult to enjoy anything. It is filled with character and characters.

Right from the time I was at school at Parramatta in Australia, I was intrigued by the information available on cricket and its participants, and I'm delighted now to be able to pen a foreword to what will be a splendid challenge to hundreds of thousands of cricket devotees. The latter, like cricketers, come in all shapes and sizes, in many different lifestyles and in all ages. There is something in this book for everyone, though whether the answers come readily is the real challenge.

The Lord's Taverners, who will be sharing in the proceeds of this book, do a marvellous job in stimulating and supporting youth cricket in all its aspects, and there is no better way to prepare for the 1985 Australian Tour of England than to browse through the following pages and see how many boundaries you can score.

Richie Benaud

Family Matters

1   Three of Bill Edrich's brothers played first-class cricket. Can you name them and the counties for which they played?

2   Gary Sobers, Clive Lloyd and Gordon Greenidge each have a cousin who has played for West Indies. Who are they?

3   Which post-war England wicket-keeper's father and son have both played county cricket?

4   Jeff and Martin Crowe are the fifth pair of brothers to appear together in a New Zealand Test side. Can you name the other four?

5   The grandfather of Ian and Greg Chappell also captained Australia. Who was he?

6   Can you name the four Mohammad brothers who have been capped for Pakistan in the order in which they made their Test debuts? And which of the four made the most Test appearances?

7   Who is the elder of the Bedser twins, Alec or Eric?

8   Which former Conservative Cabinet Minister has twin connections with Somerset?

9   Only once have a father and son each scored a hundred in the same innings of a first-class match in England. Who are they?

10   Which former England bowler is a nephew of the actor Patrick Cargill?

11   Three of Neil Harvey's brothers also played cricket for Victoria. Can you name them?

12   Which two cousins of Majid Khan have also captained Pakistan?

County Championship

The County Championship was officially constituted in 1890. Between then and 1983 . . .

1   Which county has won the most Championship titles? And how many have they won?

2   Name the four counties that have never won the Championship?

3   Which two counties have come bottom of the table the most times?

4   Only two counties have been added to the Championship Table this century. Can you name them – and the years in which they joined?

5   When did Hampshire, Warwickshire and Derbyshire last win the Championship outright?

6   Which county holds the record for the most Championship titles in succession? How many did they win, and in what years?

7   Yorkshire came bottom of the table in 1983 for the first time. What was their previous lowest position? And when?

8   Which county went from May 1935 to May 1939 without recording a single victory in a Championship match?

9   Which counties applied in 1983 to join the First-Class Championship?

10   Who won the First-Class Counties Second XI Championship in 1983?

11   Which one of the 16 first-class counties of the time did not take part in the 1919 Championship?

12   Who sponsored the Minor Counties Championship in 1983?

What's in the Middle?

Who has as his middle name:

1	Augustine	11	Sewards
2	Anderson	12	Denzil
3	St Aubrun	13	Sterling
4	Ivon	14	Isaac
5	Maitland	15	Darling
6	Christoffel	16	Fettes
7	Theophilus	17	Wendell
8	Henri	18	Orlando
9	Norris	19	Lyall
10	Middleton	20	Babulal

Poet's Corner

1   Who was 'The Surrey Poet'?

2   Whose poetry is full of *Contrasts* and *Moments and Thoughts*?

3   Which nineteenth-century English poet received a black eye from a white cricket ball?

7

Batsmen

1   Which Australian batsman scored four successive hundreds in eleven days during the 1976–7 Sheffield Shield season?

2   Who was the last batsman to score 1000 runs in May, and in what year did he perform the feat?

3   Who was the first batsman to score a hundred in both innings of the Oxford v Cambridge University Match?

4   Who was the Australian who topped the English first-class batting averages in 1953 with an average of 102?

5   Who is the only English batsman to have twice averaged over 100 in a home season?

6   Who was the first batsman to score a century for India in a Test match against Australia:
(a) Vijay Merchant (b) 'Vinoo' Mankad (c) Vijay Manjrekar?

7   Who twice scored a hundred before lunch in first-class matches in England in 1982?

8   Who in 1983 passed Don Bradman's record career-total of runs in Sheffield Shield matches?

9   Who made his Test debut in the last match of the series against West Indies in 1939, scored a total of 99 runs, but never got back into the England side after the war?

10   Who was the first to score a hundred in a Test for Pakistan?

11   Who took 142 minutes to score four runs in a County Championship match in 1974?

12   Who hit a six through the open door of the Long Room at Lord's during the England v The Dominions match in 1945, but fortunately failed to break anything?

13   Whose innings of 254 for the World XI at Melbourne in 1972 was described by Don Bradman as probably the finest ever seen in Australia?

8

14   Who made his maiden first-class century playing for Auckland against England in 1984?

15   Who was the first batsman to be dismissed for 99 on his Test debut?

16   His career-total of runs is the highest of any batsman who has not played Test cricket. Who is he?

17   Which two Australian batsmen scored centuries in each of their first two Tests, in both cases playing against England?

18   Who was the first English-born batsman to score 1000 runs in the 1983 first-class season?

19   Which West Indian batsman reached 100 off just 71 balls against Australia at Perth in 1975?

20   Who hit 72 sixes in the 1935 English season, and another 57 in the following year?

21   In which Test series against Australia did two of England's greatest batsmen average 1.25 and 4.75 respectively, and who were they?

22   Who was the first Australian batsman to score a triple century in a first-class match in England?

23   Which Essex batsman scored a century on his first-class debut in 1978?

24   Who was the first batsman to score 200 runs in boundaries in a Test match?

Mixed Cricket Bag (1)

1   Whose brother failed to win a Cup-winner's medal in the 1983 FA Cup Final?

2   Who was the first Antiguan to play Test cricket for West Indies?

3   What was Patsy Hendren's first name?

4   Which of the following teams cashed in by winning the Quaid-e-Azam Trophy, Pakistan's premier championship, in 1982–3:
(a) Allied Bank (b) Habib Bank (c) Muslim Commercial Bank (d) National Bank (e) United Bank?

5   What colour was the first uniform worn by players of the MCC?

6   Only one South African cricketer has achieved the Test double of 1000 runs and 100 wickets. Who is he?

7   When was the first women's Test match between Australia and England, and what was the result?

8   The 'Three Ws' – Everton Weekes, Frank Worrell and Clyde Walcott – were born in Barbados within 18 months of each other. Who came first?

9   Which England bowler took 200 wickets in his first full season in 1951?

10   What profession did former Test cricketers Wes Hall, Gil Langley and Clive van Ryneveld take up after retiring from the first-class game?

11   Which first-class counties since the Second World War have employed a Barker, Brazier, Carpenter, Constable, Engineer, Pope and a Pothecary?

12   Why is the hat-trick so called?

Bodyline

The controversial MCC tour of Australia in 1932–3.

1   Can you name the Australian captain and the England vice-captain?

2   Which England fast bowler refused to bowl 'bodyline'?

3   Who were the two Australian batsmen whose injuries from fast bowling caused such an outcry?

4   How many wickets did Larwood capture in the 5-Test series:
(a) 27 (b) 33 (c) 39?

5   Which Australian batsman scored 187 not out in the first Test at Sydney?

6   Who was the county captain of Larwood and Voce who encouraged 'bodyline' tactics?

7   Which two leg-spinners did England take out to Australia? And which other leg-spinner turned down an invitation to make the tour?

8   Who was the Australian fast bowler brought in for the last Test?

9   Which one of England's five pace bowlers didn't play in any of the Tests?

10   Who was the only batsman on either side to have a higher batting average than Don Bradman?

11   Did Douglas Jardine ever captain England again after the 1932–3 tour of Australia and New Zealand?

12   Which British Cabinet Minister became directly involved in the negotiations between the MCC and the Australian Board of Control over the 'bodyline' controversy?

Who said that?

Here are some memorable quotations from the world of
cricket. Do you know who said – or wrote – them?

1   Bowling on a slow wicket is rather like going out with a
thick bird. It's hard going for a while, but you get through in
the end.

2   I tend to believe that cricket is the greatest thing that
God ever created on Earth.

3   There's nowt like a game of cricket, lad. I said a game.
Cricket was never made for any championship . . . Cricket's
a game, not a competition.

4   Kerry Packer is not my style. I prefer the chugging
British coaster with a cargo of pig-iron to a monstrous
supertanker, hurriedly constructed.

5   It is the best of games, and I thank my lucky stars that
my early footsteps took me to Lord's, for, with all respect to
the other great grounds, to me it is the best place in the
world to play.

6   If the French noblesse had been capable of playing
cricket with their peasants their chateaux would never have
been burnt.

7   I remain a religious person to the delight of my parents.
I pray every night before going to sleep; occasionally I pray
for success on the field.

8   We fight the Aussies for every inch, but somehow we
keep giving the Englishmen a mile.

9   I make no pretensions to oratory, and I would any day
as soon make a duck as a speech.

10   Cricket is a well-bred game. There is no room in it for
anything but good manners. Barracking at its best is more
or less harmless; at its worst it is an absolute pestilence and
a spoil-sport.

Tests (1)

1   By a remarkable coincidence the result of the Centenary Test between Australia and England at Melbourne in 1977 was exactly the same as that of the first-ever Test between the two countries. Who won and what was the margin of victory?

2   Who was fined $200 for showing dissent at an umpire's decision during the 1st Test between West Indies and Australia in 1984?

3   Greg Chappell, Gordon Greenidge and Javed Miandad all scored a century on their Test debut. Against which countries?

4   Who holds the record for the most wickets in a Test series:
(a) Sydney Barnes (b) Jim Laker (c) Terry Alderman?

5   Which trophies are at stake in Test series between England and West Indies, and Australia and West Indies?

6   Who was the first Sri Lankan to score a Test century on home ground?

7   Who was the last England bowler to perform a hat-trick in a Test?

8   New Zealand had to wait until 1956 for their first Test victory. Who did they beat, and how many Tests had they gone without a win?

9   Who was the Pakistan opening batsman dismissed first ball on his Test debut in 1981 against Australia at Perth?

10   Which Australian batsman was dismissed for a 'pair' within 2 hours by Jim Laker at Old Trafford in 1956?

11   Five England pace bowlers made their Test debut in the series against South Africa in 1947. Can you name them?

12   How many consecutive Test appearances had Ian Botham made prior to his premature departure from Pakistan in 1984, and whose record had he equalled?

The name's the same

Each of the following pairs of cricketers share the same surname. Can you identify both players in each case?

1   (a) An England captain with a touch of class.
   (b) An Australian off-spinner and handy performer with the bat.

2   (a) An England bowler who has made more Test appearances as an umpire than as a player.
   (b) A former schoolmaster who left one Midlands county to captain another.

3   (a) He took five wickets in an innings on his Test debut for England in 1946.
   (b) A New Zealand all-rounder born in the county that (a) played for.

4   (a) He toured Australia in 1954–5 but did not play in any of the Tests.
   (b) He toured England in 1956 but did not play in any of the Tests.

5   (a) He made more than 300 consecutive County Championship appearances, and came out of retirement to help his county win the Championship for the first time.
   (b) He played in all five Tests against England in 1982–3.

6   (a) He had considerable success as a pace bowler but is best known as a bat.
   (b) A Cambridge Blue who made his debut with one of the western counties in 1980.

7   (a) He scored a match-winning double century against England at Trent Bridge in 1966.
   (b) A cousin of (a) who has since thrown in his lot with the other side.

8   (a) He never played for England and always led his county from behind.
   (b) He scored a century against Sri Lanka on his first appearance for his county.

9 (a) He took 200 wickets in a season three times.

(b) An England opener who turned out to be a Gentleman and a Player.

10 (a) He took more than 4000 wickets in league cricket.

(b) A member of an Australian touring side to England between the wars who broke his wrist on the ship coming over.

11 (a) During 1983 he was awarded his county cap and celebrated by topping his county's batting averages.

(b) A wicket-keeper who played three Tests in England in 1977 as a batsman.

12 (a) Not the jazz musician – though his slow bowling brought on the blues in a few batsmen.

(b) The nearest this all-rounder came to playing for England was when he was chosen for the ill-fated MCC tour of India, scheduled for 1939–40.

Places of Birth

Which post-war England Test cricketers were born in these foreign parts?

1   Durban (South Africa)
2   Sydney (Australia)
3   Queenstown (South Africa)
4   Simla (India)
5   Milan (Italy)
6   Wiesbaden (Germany)
7   East Point, St Philip (Barbados)
8   Kanpur (India)
9   Bulawayo (Rhodesia/Zimbabwe)
10 Lima (Peru)

Good at Games

Well-known cricketers who have made their mark in other sports.

1 He won a gold medal for fencing at the 1970 Commonwealth Games.

2 An Arsenal and England footballer who scored a century in his first Test.

3 A New Zealand cricketer who won an England rugby cap in 1947.

4 A hockey international with twelve Test caps to his name, he topped his county's batting averages in 1982.

5 He led Aston Villa to victory in the 1920 FA Cup Final.

6 He was the first to captain England at both cricket and rugby.

7 He won a gold medal at the 1908 Olympics as a middleweight boxer, though as a cricketer his batting often lacked punch.

8 A football league club which Chris Balderstone and Arnold Sidebotham have in common.

9 His last-minute penalty gave the All Blacks victory over Wales in 1978.

10 He was one of the first to bowl for England.

11 At different times Bob Willis, Graham Roope, Douglas Jardine and Percy Fender all found themselves in this position with the same club.

12 He played cricket for Kent, football for Charlton Athletic, and Great Britain at the 1952 Olympics, and later became World Fly Fishing Champion.

One-Day Internationals (excluding The World Cup)

1 Who captained England in the three-match Prudential Trophy series against Australia in 1972?

2 Which New Zealand wicket-keeper scored his one and only century in international cricket against Australia in 1974?

3 Who was the first England bowler to take five wickets in a one-day international?

4 Which batsman scored the first two centuries in one-day international cricket?

5 Who was the first New Zealand bowler to take five wickets in a one-day international?

6 Which England batsman took his first wicket in international cricket against Australia at Sydney in 1979?

7 In his only one-day international, which was also West Indies' first, he scored a duck. Who is he?

8 Who stood down from Pakistan's first game under floodlights in the 1981–2 Benson and Hedges World Series on the grounds that he would not be able to see properly when wearing glasses?

9 Who was the only Australian to score a century in the 1981–2 Benson and Hedges World Series?

10 Who was recalled to the England side at the age of 39 for the Prudential Trophy series against India in 1982?

11 England beat West Indies for the first time in a one-day international, at Headingley in 1973. How long was it before they beat them again?

12 Who was the New Zealand substitute who held four catches in a Benson and Hedges World Series match at Adelaide in 1980?

Mixed Cricket Bag (2)

1   How old was Ian Botham when Geoffrey Boycott made his Test debut?

2   Which touring side to England included the following names: Bullocky, King Cole, Tiger, Twopenny, Mosquito and Dick-a-Dick?

3   Who was the first Glamorgan cricketer to play for England?

4   Who captained Transvaal to victory in all of South Africa's major domestic competitions in 1982–3?

5   Who was the Sussex and England all-rounder who played a major part in Auckland's victory over Canterbury in the first match for the New Zealand Plunket Shield in 1907?

6   Which two young county cricketers were awarded Whitbread Scholarships to play in Australia and New Zealand in 1983–4?

7   Who was the first cricketer to complete the Australian double of 1000 runs and 50 wickets in a season?

8   On 2 February 1974, one brother was playing in a cricket Test against West Indies, while the other was playing in a rugby international against Ireland. Can you name the brothers?

9   When did the Reverend David Sheppard first play for England?

10   The Taylor twins — Mike (Hampshire) and Derek (Somerset) — had both previously been capped by a different county in each case. Can you name the two counties?

11   At Wellington in 1984 it took a maiden Test wicket by (a) to end a maiden Test hundred by (b). Who are (a) and (b)?

12   Which well-known fictional character is described by his creator as 'perhaps the very finest slow bowler of his decade'?

Hundreds and Hundreds

1 Only three players from outside England have scored 100 hundreds in first-class cricket. Who are they?

2 Who is the only batsman to have scored a double century in each innings of the same match? What match, and when?

3 Who in 1974 had the dubious honour of scoring the slowest hundred ever in English first-class cricket? And how long did it take him (in hours and minutes)?

4 The fastest century of the 1975 English season was scored against the visiting Australians. By whom, and in how many minutes?

5 Which South African batsman scored four hundreds in consecutive Test innings, the first one eight years before the other three?

6 The world record of six centuries in consecutive innings in first-class cricket is shared by three batsmen. Don Bradman is one. Can you name the other two?

7 Who in 1982 scored a century in each innings of a County Championship match with the aid of a runner?

8 How many of Jack Hobbs' 197 centuries were made after the age of 40: (a) 54 (b) 77 (c) 98?

9 In the 5th Test between West Indies and Australia in 1954–5, no less than five Australian batsmen scored centuries in the first innings – a Test record. Who were the famous five?

10 His total of 132 centuries is a record for the County Championship.

11 In 1982–3 Zaheer Abbas scored two separate hundreds in the same match for the eighth time, beating whose record?

12 Who is the only overseas player to have performed the triple feat of a century at Lord's in the University Match, Gentlemen v Players game, and a Test?

19

Captains

1   Who was the youngest county captain in 1983?

2   Who succeeded Ian Johnson as captain of Australia?

3   Who were the first modern professionals to captain Lancashire, Somerset and Worcestershire?

4   Who captained South Africa on their last visit to England in 1965?

5   In the 4th Test between England and Australia in 1968, the two opposing captains were leading their respective countries for the first and last time. Who were they?

6   Who scored a hundred in each innings of his first Test as captain in 1975?

7   Who was the last white man to captain West Indies?

8   Which are the only two counties that have not produced an England captain since the war?

9   Who captained New Zealand to their first-ever Test victory over England in 1978?

10   How many times did Middlesex win the County Championship under the captaincy of Mike Brearley?

11   Who were the first Test captains of (a) West Indies (b) India (c) Sri Lanka?

12   Who was selected to captain the MCC team to India in 1939–40, a tour that never took place because of the war?

13   In which Test series were the two opposing captains both Glamorgan players, and who were they?

14   At 23 years and 144 days he became England's youngest-ever Test captain. Who was he?

15   Which England captain was drowned at sea?

16   A. H. Kardar was Pakistan's first Test captain. Under

what name did he previously play for India?

17   There were five county captains in the England team chosen to play against South Africa at Edgbaston in 1960. Can you name them?

18   Who captained the England Young Cricketers in their three-match series against the Australian Young Cricketers in 1983?

19   Which England captain is said to have invented the position of gully?

20   Which England captain scored a century on his first appearance in first-class cricket and another on his last, 33 years later?

21   When did Jack Hobbs captain England?

22   Who captained Western Australia to win the Sheffield Shield at their first attempt in 1947–8, and what is his other main claim to fame?

23   Who took over from Sunil Gavaskar as captain of India in the last match of the series against Pakistan in 1979–80?

24   Which post-war England captain suffered from epilepsy?

Badge Spotting

1 Lancashire and Yorkshire are not the only 'Rose' counties in the Championship. Which three other counties have a rose as part of their emblem?

2 Essex and Middlesex have three each. What are they?

3 What is the Warwickshire bear holding in its paws?

4 Which county emblem stems from the narcissus?

5 What birds fly the Sussex flag – and how many are there?

6 Which fruit will you always find on display in Worcestershire?

7 What are Gloucestershire's colours?

8 What is the inscription under the white horse of Kent?

9 It has a dragon's head, wings, claws on its feet and a barbed tail. What is it?

10 What colour is the Leicestershire fox?

11 How many stars are there on the West Indies' badge?

12 What is holding what for Sri Lanka?

Anagrams

Each of the following is an anagram of a famous cricketer's name. How many of the six can you identify?

1 I'M THE KILLER (5, 6)
2 BRASSY OGRE (4, 6)
3 VERY SAFE DONG (7, 5)
4 CANCELS RAIN (5, 6)
5 HON SANK HIM (6, 4)
6 BE A TORY LIVER (6, 6)

22

The Doc and the Don (Dr W. G. Grace and Don Bradman)

1 What was Grace's favourite cricketing headgear?

2 In 1885 Grace scored 221 not out for Gloucestershire against Middlesex at Clifton. Was it after:
(a) having been up all night with a patient?
(b) being bitten on the leg by a dog?
(c) walking 20 miles to the ground from his home?

3 How old was Grace when he first captained England?

4 Who clean bowled Grace the most times in first-class cricket?

5 What life-saving act did Grace perform on the cricket field in 1887?

6 What was Grace's reported fee for captaining Lord Sheffield's team to Australia in 1891?

7 What was the name of the town where Don Bradman was born?

8 How many times in first-class cricket did Bradman score over 300 runs in an innings?

9 Playing for South Australia against NSW in 1938, Bradman did something for the first and only time in his first-class career. What was it?

10 England aside, in what other countries (overseas) did Bradman play Test cricket?

11 How many times was Bradman dismissed for a duck in Tests?

12 What almost killed Bradman during the 1934 tour of England?

Mixed Cricket Bag (3)

1   Who made his Test debut in 1983–4 against Pakistan in what was only his twelfth first-class match?

2   They both batted right-handed, bowled left and came from Kirkheaton. Who are they?

3   Who was the first black cricketer to take part in a tour of South Africa?

4   For which teams in the Caribbean Shell Shield Competition did the following play in 1982–3: Wayne Daniel, Eldine Baptiste, Augustine Logie and Winston Davis?

5   Which team was beaten in the 1981–2 Ranji Trophy Final in India after having scored 705 in their first innings?

6   Can you place these English cricketing 'flora and fauna': Bear, Catt, Crabtree, Hazell, Peach, Oakes, Roe, Root and Vine?

7   What momentous event in the world of cricket took place in 1848?

8   Who was the first cricketer to achieve the double of 100 runs and ten wickets in the same Test match?

9   How did Bob Willis break the news to Neil Foster that he would not be playing in the 2nd Test against New Zealand at Christchurch in 1984?

10   What was the name of the West Indian batsman whose dismissal (run out) at Georgetown in 1954 triggered off the infamous bottle-throwing incident?

11   Who were the winners of the Whitbread Village Championship Trophy in 1983?

12   According to the laws of the game, in how many ways can a batsman be dismissed – and what are they?

Answers on p 69–70

Record Holders

1 Who was the first to score 2000 runs and take 200 wickets in Tests?

2 Who holds the record for taking the longest amount of time (97 minutes) to get off the mark in a first-class match?

3 Who was the only man to play first-class cricket in England before the First World War and after the Second?

4 Who has bowled the most deliveries (27115) in Test cricket?

5 Who is the only batsman to have scored five centuries in a Test series, and to have made two separate hundreds in a Test twice in the same rubber?

6 Who in 1963 became the youngest bowler ever to take 100 wickets in an English first-class season?

7 Which two New Zealand batsmen share the world record of two double-century opening stands in the same match?

8 Who was the first to achieve the triple feat of 1000 runs, 100 wickets and 100 catches in Test matches?

9 Who holds the record for hitting the most sixes (15) in a single first-class innings?

10 Who is the only bowler to have taken 100 wickets in an English season on 20 consecutive occasions?

11 Who is the only player to have achieved the double of 1000 runs and 100 wickets in his maiden first-class season?

12 Who is the only player to have bagged four pairs of ducks in Test cricket:
(a) A. L. Valentine (b) B. S. Chandrasekhar (c) Iqbal Qasim?

Tests (2)

1   Who was England's first Test captain?

2   How many England bowlers have taken 200 Test wickets, and who are they?

3   In the 'Tied Test' at Brisbane in 1960, who was the West Indian fieldsman who ran out two of Australia's last four batsmen in the final dramatic overs of the match?

4   Who is the only England player to have scored a century at Lord's on his Test debut?

5   Which Australian spinner bowled a spell of 51 overs against England at Old Trafford in 1964?

6   New Zealand played Australia for the first time in a Test match in 1946. How long was it before the two countries met again in an official Test?

7   In the Edgbaston Test against India in 1974, Sunil Gavaskar was given out to the first ball of the match, caught behind off the bowling of Geoff Arnold. The umpire faced with such an early decision was making his Test debut. Who was he?

8   Who carried his bat through Australia's first innings against England at Lord's in 1926, scoring 193 not out in a total of 383?

9   Throughout his long innings of 220 for India against West Indies at Port-of-Spain in 1971, Sunil Gavaskar was in considerable pain. Why?

10   Only two England cricketers have scored a century on their Test debut, when that debut was against Australia in England. W. G. Grace is one. Who is the other?

11   Which Australian batsman was given out 'handling the ball' in the 2nd Test against Pakistan at Perth in 1979?

12   Who were the last two batsmen at the wicket for England before the Second World War was declared?

Limited Overs

1   The first Gillette Cup final was between Sussex and Worcestershire in 1963. Who was Man of the Match?

2   Who were the first players in a Gillette Cup final to (a) score a hundred (b) take five wickets?

3   Who scored the first-ever century in the Gillette Cup competition:
(a) Maurice Hallam (b) Peter Marner (c) Eric Russell?

4   After 20 years of limited-overs cricket, which was the only first-class county never to have played in a cup final at Lord's?

5   Who were the two batsmen at the wicket when Derbyshire 'tied' with Northamptonshire in the 1981 NatWest final?

6   A record number of sixes was struck in John Player League matches in 1982. Were there:
(a) 541 (b) 588 (c) 619?

7   Which county lost a John Player League match in 1982 after batting first and scoring 299 for 4 in their 40 overs?

8   Which batsman hit the most sixes in the John Player League in 1983?

9   Who were the losing finalists in the first Benson and Hedges Cup competition in 1972?

10   Who performed a hat-trick in the 1974 Benson and Hedges Cup final?

11   Who were the first to win the John Player League Trophy two years running?

12   Who won the Gold Award for the 1982 Benson and Hedges Cup final?

13   The biggest-ever hit in a Gillette Cup final sent the ball into the guttering at the top of the Lord's pavilion. Who was

the batsman – and the bowler? When was it, and who won the Cup?

14   Which was the first minor county to defeat a first-class county in the Gillette Cup? And who did they beat?

15   Who led Tasmania to victory in the Australian Gillette Cup competition in 1978–9?

16   Whose innings of 198 not out in a Benson and Hedges match in 1982 was the highest score ever made in a limited-overs game in Britain?

17   Who were the winners of the South African Datsun Shield three years running (1978–9, 79–80, 80–1)?

18   Who was the first cricketer to play for four counties in the John Player League, and which counties were they?

19   The first hat-trick in the Gillette Cup competition was performed by a Northamptonshire bowler in 1963. Who was he?

20   Who was the only bowler to take eight wickets in a John Player League match prior to 1984?

21   Who were the Australian Gillette Cup winners who beat the MCC in a limited-overs match at Melbourne in 1975?

22   In a Benson and Hedges match against Derbyshire in 1981, two Yorkshire batsmen put on a record last wicket stand of 80 runs. Seventy-six of these were scored by one batsman. Who was he? Can you name his partner? And what was the result of the match?

23   Which Somerset bowler had figures of 8–8–0–0 in a John Player League match in 1969?

24   Which county won their first-ever trophy at Lord's in 1976, and what was it?

Around the Grounds

1   Where are these Test match grounds: (a) Carisbrook
(b) Kensington Oval (c) St George's Park (d) Feroz Shah
Kotla (e) Recreation Ground?

2   Where, in the words of Neville Cardus, was it 'always
afternoon and 304 for 2'?

3   Who would be the home side in an international match
at Churchill Park?

4   Where was Leicestershire's main ground from 1901 to
1939?

5   How many people does the Melbourne Cricket Ground
hold?

6   Which Yorkshire ground staged its one and only Test
match in 1902?

7   Which ground did John Arlott have in mind when he
wrote:

> From the top of the hill-top pavilion
> The sea is a cheat to the eye,
> Where it secretly seeps into coastline
> Or fades in the yellow-grey sky ...

8   Middlesex CCC took up residence at Lord's in 1877.
Where had they been based for the five years before that?

9   What was the venue for Sri Lanka's first-ever Test
match, in February 1982?

10   Where was the original county ground of Essex?

11   Where in New Zealand in 1979 was a Test match
played for the first time?

12   What is 'The Gabba' short for?

Cricketing Dates

The answer is the year in each case.

1 When did the MCC come into being?

2 When was the start of the John Player League competition?

3 When was the last Gentlemen v Players match?

4 When was the first series of 5-day Test matches in England?

5 When did England begin two Test matches on the same day?

6 When was overarm bowling legalised?

7 When was the first Test match in England with play on a Sunday?

8 When did W. G. Grace's Test career end and Wilfred Rhodes' begin?

9 When did England play its first Test match against (a) West Indies (b) New Zealand (c) India (d) Pakistan?

10 When was the first edition of *Wisden Cricketers' Almanack* published?

11 When was the Test and County Cricket Board (TCCB) formed?

12 When was the first match played at the present Lord's ground?

Cricketing Nobs

Can you identify the following titled cricketers?

1   He toured New Zealand with the MCC side in 1935–6, later returning there as Governor General.

2   His autobiography was entitled *From Verse to Worse*.

3   Towards the end of his life he was created Baron of Maraval and Nelson.

4   Younger son of Lord Rochester, he topped his county's bowling averages in 1980.

5   Captain of England was just one of the parts he played.

6   He was knighted for his services to cricket in 1953.

7   He bequeathed The Ashes to the MCC.

8   A prince among English batsmen, he married Princess Jayrajkumari of Rajpipla.

9   He led England to victory in a Test series against Australia, heading both the batting and the bowling averages.

10   He wrote a calypso celebrating West Indies' first-ever Test victory in England.

11   A hot-blooded Irishman who captained England and once threatened to fight W. G. Grace at the wicket.

12   Captain of the Indian side which toured England in 1936.

Mixed Cricket Bag (4)

1   Who was flown out to join the England team in Pakistan in 1978 after Mike Brearley had suffered a broken arm?

2   What was unusual about the player who topped the English first-class bowling averages in 1908?

3   Which two Yorkshire cricketers were awarded their county caps along with Geoffrey Boycott in 1963?

4   What musical instrument did the Leicestershire and England all-rounder W. E. Astill play?

5   Which team came bottom of the Caribbean Shell Shield Table in 1983–4?

6   What trophy was at stake in the 1984 series between New Zealand and England?

7   In 1896 five England professionals threatened to withdraw from the Test side to play Australia at The Oval unless they were paid twice their usual match fee. Who were they – and how much were they demanding to be paid?

8   In what way did the Indian touring side to England in 1946 make history on their arrival?

9   For how many seasons did London County have first-class status?

10   Who was the first bowler to perform a hat-trick in a Test match?

11   Who chewed gum for the first time as an aid to concentration while batting in the 3rd Test between New Zealand and England at Auckland in 1984 and finished up with a century and an aching jaw?

12   A 'very singular' game of cricket was advertised in a Kent newspaper in 1794, between the Gentlemen of the Hill and the Gentlemen of the Dale for 1 guinea a man. Was it to be played:
(a) in fancy dress (b) on horseback (c) with each player having one arm tied behind his back?

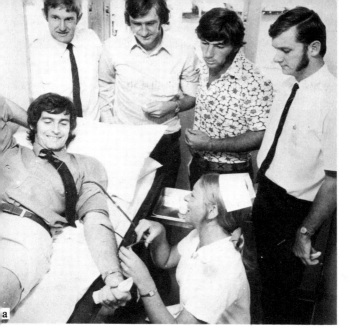

Can you identify these well-known cricketers shown here in somewhat unfamiliar circumstances? *(Answers on pp. 75–76.)*

2 (a) The fieldsman nearest the camera has just narrowly missed running out the batsman on the ground. Who are they – and can you name the other players in the picture?
(b) Who is the unlucky batsman with his two outside stumps uprooted? And who was the bowler who performed this remarkable feat?

3 Who are these two batsmen – and do you recognise the wicket-keeper and fieldsman in each case?

4   Can you put a name to these two sons of famous
    cricketing fathers?

5 Batting is not the first thing you associate with these two cricketers. Who are they?

a

6 Can you identify these three spin bowlers, all of whom played Test cricket after World War II?

b

c

7 Who are these three wildly expressive fast bowlers from 'Down Under' who toured England during the Sixties and Seventies?

8 Who are Viv Richards (a) and Geoffrey Boycott (b) congratulating? And why?

Bowlers

1 Which two bowlers took five wickets in an innings nine times in first-class matches in England in 1983?

2 Which Australian fast bowler was no-balled 35 times at Worcester in 1938, playing in his first match in England?

3 In the exhibition match which followed the 2nd Test at Lord's in 1960, the South African fast bowler Geoff Griffen was no-balled for two different offences. The first was for throwing. What was the second?

4 Who put himself on against Surrey in 1955 as a change bowler and ended up taking 8 for 0 in 12 overs?

5 The first bowler to take 200 wickets in Tests was a New Zealander. What was his name?

6 What is 'Venkat' short for?

7 Who was the last bowler to take ten wickets in an innings in a first-class match in England?

8 Who was the first Pakistan bowler to take 100 Test wickets?

9 Who took 4 wickets in 4 balls, 5 in 6 balls, 6 in 9 balls, and 7 in 11 balls in a world record-breaking spell in 1972?

10 Which Northamptonshire pace bowler in 1961 twice performed the hat-trick in County Championship matches within the space of six weeks?

11 Who was the 16-year-old Pakistan spin bowler who took a match-winning 6–67 against West Indies in the 5th Test at Port-of-Spain in 1958?

12 Which England fast bowler was forced to return home early from the 1970–1 tour of Australia because of injury?

13 Who was the only bowler in 1982 to capture 100 wickets in first-class cricket in England?

14 With what name did the Australian fast bowler Len Pascoe start out in life?

15   Who took 100 wickets in a season 12 times, 9 wickets in an innings twice, 8 wickets in an innings 6 times, and 7 wickets in an innings 15 times, but never played for England?

16   In 1955 Fred Titmus set a new Middlesex record by taking 158 wickets in the season. Whose record did he beat?

17   Who were the two Leicestershire players who bowled unchanged through four consecutive innings of County Championship matches in 1935?

18   Who developed a unique method of spinning the ball while stationed in New Guinea during the Second World War?

19   Who performed a hat-trick in both innings of a County Championship match against Surrey in 1949?

20   Who was the South African Test spinner who died in December 1983 at the age of 51?

21   The legendary Australian fast bowler Ted McDonald died in England in 1937 in somewhat bizarre circumstances. What were they?

22   With which county did the great Surrey fast bowler Tom Richardson end his first-class career?

23   Who was England's leading wicket-taker in the 1965–6 series against Australia?

24   Which two Australian bowlers in the 1931–2 domestic season achieved the rare distinction of clean bowling Don Bradman for a duck?

Partners

1   Who was Geoffrey Boycott's opening partner in the 1965–6 Test series against Australia?

2   Who was Alec Bedser's opening partner in the 1948–9 Test series against South Africa?

3   Which opening pair established an all-Tests record in 1956 with their 1st-wicket partnership of 413, and whose record did they beat?

4   Between them this well-known spinning duo took 4761 wickets in first-class cricket, but the sum total of their Test appearances was only nine. Who are they?

5   Which two Lancashire batsmen in 1978 put on 234 for the 4th wicket in a Gillette Cup match – the highest partnership for any wicket in the competition – and who were they playing against?

6   Who were the members of the South African 'googly quartet' who toured England in 1907?

7   What was the difference in age between Jack Hobbs and Herbert Sutcliffe when they first opened the innings together for England?

8   How many batsmen in Test matches fell to the 'c Marsh b Lillee' combination?

9   When Geoffrey Boycott and John Edrich scored their 100th hundreds in 1977 they each had the same batting partner at the other end. Who was he, and in what matches were these two milestones reached?

10   In the 1st Test against West Indies at Bridgetown in 1935, the same pair opened the batting and bowling for England. Can you name them?

11   Which three Indian batsmen added 415 for the 3rd wicket against England in the 5th Test at Madras in 1982?

12   Can you add the other half to these successful county partnerships: (a) Shackleton and . . . (b) Keeton and . . . (c) Flavell and . . . (d) Tribe and . . . (e) Robertson and . . . (f) Butler and . . . (g) Washbrook and . . . (h) Underwood and . . .

Initial Questions

Can you add the surnames to the following sets of initials?
Give yourself bonus points if you know what they stand for
as well.

1	KWR	11	EAE
2	RGD	12	PWG
3	IVA	13	APE
4	DVP	14	APF
5	LEG	15	NEJ
6	AME	16	JHB
7	RDV	17	JRT
8	GAR	18	GOB
9	RWV	19	NFM
10	GHG	20	GRJ

Anagrams

More anagrams of famous cricketers' names.

1 DEAR RACHEL HID (7, 6)

2 WARTIME CORN (6, 5)

3 I BOWL LIBS (3, 6)

4 LAUGH, DEFY, HIT (4, 8)

5 SWEET, KEEN OVER (7, 6)

6 BREEDS RICE; BREEDS LACE (4, 6; 4, 6)

44

Who's Who

1   Who failed to win the Cardiff South East seat for the Conservatives in the 1964 General Election?

2   Who were known as the 'Lion of Kent' and the 'Lion of the North'?

3   Who was refused permission to use a blue-coloured bat in the Lord's Test against New Zealand in 1973? .

4   Who asked to be buried 22 yards from another famous Test cricketer, 'so I can send him down a ball now and then'? And who was the 'batsman'?

5   Who managed to be the England Chairman of Selectors and cricket correspondent of the *Morning Post* at the same time?

6   Who was named after two Australian aviators?

7   Who was elected President of the Cricketers' Association in 1968?

8   Who was the first woman cricketer to be the subject of a special feature in *Wisden*?

9   Who was F. S. Jackson's fag at Harrow?

10   Who started life at 14lb 1oz and finished up a cricketing giant?

11   Who got so steamed up he could never play cricket again?

12   Who invented a mechanical bowling machine called the 'Catapulta'?

13   Who was the manager of the 1946–7 MCC side which toured Australia?

14   Who was Ray Illingworth's best man?

15   Who was stopped from getting to the throne by a cricket ball?

16   Who was refused re-entry to Pakistan in 1983 after a Sam 7 missile was allegedly discovered under his bed at home there?

17   Who carried the bags for England after he had taken the gloves off?

18   Who in 1841 issued an order to the effect that every military barracks should have a cricket ground constructed alongside?

19   Who called his autobiography *Batting from Memory*?

20   Who is the National Cricket Association's Director of Coaching?

21   Who was banned from playing for his county ever again after coming on to the field drunk and relieving himself in front of his captain?

22   Who was sent home in disgrace for bowling 'beamers'?

23   Who went on show at Madame Tussaud's in London in the summer of 1982?

24   Who was the first President of the United States of America to watch Test cricket?

Weights and Measures

1   How much should a regulation cricket ball weigh when new?

2   Which modification to the rules of the NatWest Competition in 1982 caused more than a few players to lose sleep?

3   Which county in the 1983 Schweppes Championship clocked the best hourly over rate, and which clocked the worst?

4   What is the longest recorded distance that a bail has travelled after a batsman has been bowled in a first-class match:
(a) 46yd 11in (b) 67yd 6in (c) 83yd 2in?

5   What was the amount of Jack Simmons' benefit in 1980?

6   If you laid Joel Garner and Vintcent van der Bijl end to end, what would be the distance between the two ends?

7   Which of the major English cricket grounds has the largest playing area, and how large is it (to the nearest acre)?

8   Sir Pelham Warner described the slope at Lord's which runs from the Grandstand boundary down to the Tavern boundary as being 'about the height of a tall man in a top hat'. What in fact is the difference in height between the two boundaries?

9   Six-ball overs have been the rule in English first-class cricket since 1900, except for one season when eight-ball overs were tried. Was it in:
(a) 1919 (b) 1929 (c) 1939?

10   How wide is the regulation cricket pitch?

11   Which county in the 1983 Schweppes Championship recorded the fastest run rate per 100 balls, and which recorded the slowest?

12   Who was sponsored to the tune of 1 dollar a run in the 1970–1 season while playing for South Australia?

Overseas Players in England

1 For which first-class counties did the following post-war Test cricketers play: J. W. Guy (NZ), K. Miller (Australia), A. A. Baig (India), P. L. Winslow (S Africa), Khan Mohammad (Pakistan)?

2 Which school do Viv Richards and Andy Roberts have in common?

3 In 1949 this New Zealand fast bowler took 113 wickets in the English season, though he wasn't a member of the NZ touring side of that year. Who was he, and for whom did he play?

4 Danny was one, Jock was almost another. Who are they?

5 He topped his county's bowling averages in 1981 and 1982, and scored the fastest century of the 1981 season in 62 minutes. Who is he?

6 Who found himself in the limelight via Fleetwood and Gloucestershire in 1981?

7 This South African batsman hit 26 sixes in his first season with Essex.

8 Can you name the Australian all-rounder who completed the double of 1000 runs and 100 wickets on eight occasions, and five times performed the hat-trick, but never played Test cricket?

9 Who took a record 208 wickets for Cambridge University between 1954–7?

10 Five cricketers have played in Test matches for both England and Australia. Can you name them and the English first-class counties for which they played?

11 'A' took 101 wickets in 1980, 'B' was the only batsman to top 2000 runs in 1982. They were both playing for the same county. Who are they?

12 Which Australian father and son have played for Somerset?

Answers on p 82–3

World Cup

1   One of the most prolific batsmen of all time, he took 60 overs to score just 36 runs in the opening match of the Prudential World Cup competition in 1975. Who is he?

2   Which two non-Test playing countries took part in the first World Cup competition?

3   Which Australian bowler took five wickets in the 1975 final?

4   Which two England batsmen scored a century in the 1975 competition, and who was the only batsman from any country to score two centuries?

5   Who is the only batsman in any of the three Prudential World Cup competitions to have scored a century before lunch?

6   Who were the four semi-finalists in the ICC tournament which preceded the 1979 World Cup?

7   Who pulled out of the 1978 ICC tournament and were replaced by Wales?

8   How did Viv Richards end his innings in the 1979 final against England?

9   Who was England's top scorer in the 1979 final?

10   How many of Joel Garner's five victims in the 1979 final were clean bowled?

11   Which England player was twice voted Man of the Match in the 1979 competition?

12   Who holds the record for the best bowling performance in all Prudential World Cup matches, and how many wickets did he take?

13   Who captured the vital wicket of Viv Richards in the 1983 final?

14   How many of Kapil Dev's 175 not out against Zimbabwe in 1983 came in boundaries?

15   Which spin bowler won two Man of the Match awards in the 1983 competition?

16   Who was the first to win a Man of the Match award for Zimbabwe?

17   Which team in the 1975 competition had two of its leading batsmen hospitalised by Jeff Thomson, and who were the injured parties?

18   Which England cricketer's father played in the 1975 competition – against England?

19   How many Australian batsmen were run out in the 1975 final?

20   Which team in the 1979 competition included seven players who were West Indian-born? (Besides West Indies, that is.)

21   Which country set a new record in 1983 for a side batting second in the competition?

22   Which England player won the Man of the Match award against Sri Lanka at Headingley in 1983, and why?

23   The prize money for the winners of the Cup in 1975 was the same as that for the losing finalists in 1979. How much was it?

24   How many of the beaten West Indian finalists of 1983 played in the 1979 final, and who were they?

Accidents will Happen

1   John Edrich, Bert Sutcliffe, Nari Contractor, Jackie Hendricks and Graeme Watson were all badly injured when hit on the head by deliveries from fast bowlers. Who were the bowlers in each case?

2   Who broke whose arm in the Lord's Test of 1963?

3   Car accidents 33 years apart tragically destroyed the careers of two Northamptonshire and England batsmen. Who are they, and in what years did the accidents happen?

4   Who almost choked to death on a piece of gum after being hit on the heart by a ball from Bob Willis?

5   Which Australian player broke his ankle bowling leg breaks at The Oval in 1938?

6   Who gave Ewen Chatfield the kiss of life at Auckland in 1975, after he had been struck on the temple by a ball while batting? And who was the bowler?

7   Which three cricketers continued their Test careers after accidents had resulted in (a) the left arm being shortened by 2 inches (b) the loss of four toes (c) blindness in the right eye?

8   New Zealander John Wright managed to run out two of his fellow countrymen in the Headingley Test of 1983. Who were they?

9   Which England fast bowler at Old Trafford in 1948 put Australian opener Sid Barnes into hospital for 10 days?

10   Who broke whose jaw in the 1976 Centenary Test?

11   Which West Indian cricketer was born with an extra finger on each hand, necessitating an operation to remove them when he was a child?

12   Batting in a county match for Gloucestershire against Northants in 1961, Tom Pugh ducked into a ball from David Larter and had his jaw broken in two places. He was promptly given out by the umpire. On what grounds?

51

Tests (3)

1   Who took seven wickets for one run in the space of 33 deliveries in a Test match in 1979?

2   Who was the first England player to score a century and take five wickets in an innings in the same Test?

3   The Australian batsman W. H. Ponsford scored 181 and 266 in consecutive innings against England in 1934. On each occasion he was dismissed in the same way. How was that?

4   Which Indian bowler conceded just five runs in 32 overs during the Madras Test against England in 1964?

5   Who was Zaheer Abbas' runner during his innings of 82 not out against England at Lahore in 1984?

6   What was unusual about one of the umpires for the 3rd Test between West Indies and Australia in 1965?

7   How many of Australia's first-ever Test team were born in England, and who were they?

8   Which England batsman made his Test debut against West Indies at Edgbaston in 1963, top-scoring with 85 not out in the second innings?

9   Who wrapped up South Africa's second innings in the 4th Test at Headingley in 1947 by taking the last four wickets in one over?

10   What do Maurice Tate, Dick Howarth and Intikhab Alam have in common?

11   Who set a record for all Test matches by hitting six boundaries (all fours) in one over against England at Old Trafford in 1982? And who was the unfortunate bowler?

12   Whose nine-hour-long innings of 137 not out enabled England to force a draw against India at Delhi in 1951?

Behind the Stumps

1   Who claimed his 1000th victim in first-class cricket in 1959?

2   How old was Wally Grout when he first played for Australia?

3   Who was the first wicket-keeper to score a hundred in Anglo-Australian Tests, and in what year was it?

4   Who claimed the most dismissals in the 1983 English season?

5   Who was the first wicket-keeper to claim 100 dismissals in Anglo-Australian Tests?

6   Who kept wicket for India in the three Tests against England in 1946?

7   In how many Test matches did Roger Tolchard keep wicket for England?

8   The world record of 12 dismissals in a first-class match was established by the Surrey wicket-keeper, Ted Pooley, in 1868. Which two Australians have equalled it?

9   Who holds the record for the most stumpings in a single innings of a first-class match, and what is the number?

10   Who is the only wicket-keeper to score a century and claim six dismissals in an innings in the same Test match?

11   Who was the New Zealand wicket-keeper who played for the Gentlemen against the Players in 1958?

12   Which former captain of Australia kept wicket for England, and when?

13   Which Australian wicket-keeper was a Yorkshireman by birth and an undertaker by trade?

14   Who was the first wicket-keeper to score 4000 runs in Tests?

15 Who shared with Rodney Marsh the one-time world record of 26 dismissals in a Test series?

16 Who donned the gloves for England in Australia's second innings at The Oval in 1934, and what record did he establish?

17 Who was the Pakistan wicket-keeper who managed not to concede a single bye during England's innings of 544 for 5 in the Edgbaston Test of 1962?

18 Who kept wicket in a Test match against his own countrymen in 1956?

19 Who replaced Rodney Marsh in the Australian Test side after the latter had joined World Series Cricket?

20 Leslie Ames achieved the double of 1000 runs and 100 dismissals in an English season on three occasions. Who is the only other wicket-keeper to have completed this double?

21 Can you identify these three wicket-keepers currently playing county cricket?

'A' has a degree in biological sciences

'B' is a former policeman

'C' keeps ferrets

22 Who kept wicket for West Indies in the first three Tests against England in 1957?

23 Who holds the record for the most stumpings in Test cricket?

24 What do Anil Dalpat and Syed Kirmani have in common, though they are not the same?

Mixed Cricket Bag (5)

1 Which Australian batsman scored his maiden Test century against West Indies at Sabina Park in 1978, following it up with 97 in the second innings?

2 For which other country did the New Zealand Test cricketer C. S. Dempster play?

3 What was The Oval before it was turned into a cricket ground in 1845?

4 Who was the first woman cricketer to hit a six in a Test match:
(a) Betty Snowball (b) Rachel Heyhoe-Flint (c) Molly Hide?

5 Which post-war England captain's school report contained the following comment: 'He shows promise at cricket but he must remember he has still much – in fact almost everything – to learn and is not yet in a position to control and give instructions to his fellows, who quite rightly resent it'?

6 What is a 'bunsen'?

7 Who was England's last lob bowler?

8 Which member of the 1984 England touring side to New Zealand and Pakistan had previously been employed as a real-tennis professional and glassblower?

9 Where, in 1867, did the MCC play their first match outside Britain?

10 Which famous spin bowler of recent years made his first-class debut at 15, having only seriously started to play cricket two years earlier?

11 Whose Test hat-trick was not only the first-ever for his side, but also the first on an Easter Sunday?

12 What did the head groundsman fish out of the flooded Worcester ground in 1934:
(a) a 45lb salmon (b) three swan's eggs (c) a grand piano?

ANSWERS

Family Matters

1 Eric (E. H.), Lancs

Geoffrey (G. A.), Lancs

Brian (B. R.), Kent and Glam.

2 David Holford, Lance Gibbs, Andy Roberts.

3 Jim Parks'. His father, J. H. Parks, played for Sussex and England; his son, R. J. Parks, plays for Hants.

4 Brendon and John Bracewell

Dayle and Richard Hadlee

Geoffrey and Hedley Howarth

John and Norman Parker.

5 Victor Richardson.

6 Hanif, Wazir, Mushtaq, Sadiq.

Mushtaq 57 (two more than Hanif).

7 Eric.

8 Geoffrey Rippon. His father (A. E. S. Rippon) and uncle (A. D. E. Rippon), who were twins, both played for the county.

9 George Gunn and George Vernon Gunn (for Notts v Warks, 1931).

10 Robin Jackman.

11 Mervyn, Clarrie, Ray.

12 Javed Burki, Imran Khan.

County Championship

1 Yorks 30 (29 outright, 1 shared).

2 Gloucs, Northants, Somerset, Sussex.

3 Derbys and Northants (11 times each).

4 Northants 1905, Glam 1921.

5 1973, 1972, 1936.

6 Surrey 7 (1952–8).

7 14th in 1973.

8 Northants.

9 Shropshire, Northumberland & Durham (as one).

10 Leics.

11 Worcs.

12 United Friendly Insurance.

What's in the Middle

1	John Snow	11	Fred Trueman
2	Barry Richards	12	Malcolm Marshall
3	Gary Sobers	13	Garth Le Roux
4	David Gower	14	Alvin Kallicharran
5	Glenn Turner	15	John Inchmore
6	Kepler Wessels	16	Brian Davison
7	Sylvester Clarke	17	Wayne Daniel
8	Phillippe Edmonds	18	Roland Butcher
9	Wilf Slack	19	Chris Smith
10	Chris Old	20	Rohan Kanhai

Poet's Corner

1 Albert Craig – a Yorkshireman who became famous through selling his cricketing verse at The Oval around the turn of the century. He died in 1909.

2 John Snow's. These are the titles of his two published volumes of poetry.

3 John Keats in 1819. He recorded the incident in a letter to a friend.

Batsmen

1 David Hookes (S Australia): 185 and 105 v Queensland; 135 and 156 v NSW.

2 Charles Hallows, 1928 (5–31 May).

3 R. J. Boyd-Moss; for Cambridge, 1983 (139 and 124).

4 Fast bowler W. A. Johnston, who was not out 16 times in 17 innings for the touring Australians.

5 Geoffrey Boycott (1971, 1979).

6 'Vinoo' Mankad; 116 at Melbourne, 1948.

7 Glenn Turner (Worcs) v Warks and Lancs.

8 John Inverarity (S Australia). Bradman scored his 8926 runs in 96 innings (ave: 110.20); Inverarity took 258 innings (ave: 39.99).

9 Norman Oldfield (Lancs and Northants).

10 Nazar Mohammad (father of Mudassar Nazar), who scored 124 not out v India at Lucknow in 1952. Nazar, who went in first, carried his bat through the completed innings. Pakistan won by an innings and 43 runs in what was only their second official Test.

11 Brian Hardie (Essex) v Hants.

12 Walter Hammond.

13   Gary Sobers'.

14   John Bracewell; 104 not out.

15   A. G. Chipperfield (Australia) v England at Trent Bridge, 1934.

16   Alan Jones (Glam). Between 1957–83 he scored 36024 runs in first-class cricket. He played for England once v Rest of the World in 1970, but the match does not rate as an official Test.

17   W. H. Ponsford (1924–5); K. D. Walters (1965–6).

18   Mark Nicholas (Hants).

19   Roy Fredericks, who opened the innings. He was finally out for 169, scored off 145 balls in 212 minutes.

20   Arthur Wellard (Somerset), who also twice hit five consecutive sixes in a first-class match.

21   1902; C. B. Fry and K. S. Ranjitsinhji. They each played in three Tests but only had four innings. Fry's scores were 0, 0, 1, 4. Ranji's were 13, 0, 2, 4.

22   Victor Trumper; 300 not out for Australians v Sussex, 1899.

23   Alan Lilley; 100 not out v Notts.

24   John Edrich v New Zealand at Headingley in 1965. His innings of 310 included 5 sixes and 52 fours.

Mixed Cricket Bag (1)

1   Mike Gatting's (Steve Gatting played for Brighton, the losing finalists).

2   Andy Roberts, 1974 (v England).

3   Elias.

4   (e) United Bank.

5   Sky blue.

6   Trevor Goddard (2516 runs, 123 wickets).

7   1934 at Brisbane. England won by 9 wickets.

8   Frank Worrell, 1 August 1924.

9   Bob Appleyard (Yorks); his 200 wickets cost 14.14 runs apiece.

10   Politics.

11   Essex, Surrey and Kent, Gloucs, Surrey, Lancs, Derbys, Hants.

12   In earlier days a hat was presented to any bowler taking three wickets with consecutive balls. The first recorded instance of a hat being awarded under such circumstances was in 1858.

Bodyline

1   W. M. Woodfull, R. E. S. Wyatt.

2   G. O. Allen.

3   W. M. Woodfull, W. A. Oldfield.

4   33 (ave: 19.51).

5   Stan McCabe.

6   A. W. Carr.

7   F. R. Brown and T. B. Mitchell; Walter Robins.

8   H. H. Alexander.

9   Maurice Tate.

10   Eddie Paynter.

11   Yes (v West Indies 1933 and India 1933–4).

12   J. H. Thomas, Dominions Secretary.

Who said that?

1   Jeff Thomson.

2   Harold Pinter.

3   George Hirst.

4   Mike Brearley.

5   Denis Compton (from *Denis Compton: A Cricket Sketch* by E. W. Swanton).

6   George Macaulay Trevelyan.

7   Vivian Richards (quoted in *Viv Richards* by David Foot).

8   Richard Hadlee.

9   W. G. Grace.

10   Frank Woolley (from *The King of Games*).

Tests (1)

1   Australia won by 45 runs.

2   Geoff Lawson – by the Australian authorities.

3   (a) 108 v England, 1970–1.
     (b) 107 v India, 1974–5.
     (c) 163 v New Zealand, 1976–7.

4   Sydney Barnes; 49 v S Africa, 1913–14.

5   The Wisden Trophy and the Frank Worrell Trophy.

6   R. L. Diaz; 108 v New Zealand at Colombo, 1984.

7   Peter Loader; v West Indies at Headingley, 1957. His final figures were 6–36.

8   West Indies by 190 runs. 44.

9   Rizwan-uz-Zaman.

10   Neil Harvey (2 of Laker's 19 wickets in the match).

11   J. W. Martin (Kent); G. H. Pope (Derbys); C. Gladwin (Derbys); K. Cranston (Lancs); H. J. Butler (Notts).

12   65. Alan Knott's.

The Name's the Same

1   Yardley: Norman (Yorks) and Bruce (W Australia).

2   Palmer: Ken (Somerset) and Charles (Worcs to Leics).

3   Pollard: Dick (Lancs) and Vic (Central Districts).

4   Wilson: Vic (Yorks) and Jack (S Australia).

5   Dyson: Arnold (Glam) and John (NSW).

6   Surridge: Stuart (Surrey) and David (Gloucs).

7   Butcher: Basil (Guyana) and Roland (Middx).

8   Taylor: Brian (Essex) and Neil (Kent).

9   Richardson: Tom (Surrey) and Peter (Worcs/Kent).

10   Barnes: Sydney (Warks/Staffs/Lancs) and Sidney (NSW).

11   Robinson: Tim (Notts) and Richard (Victoria).

12   Parker: Charlie (Gloucs) and Jack (Surrey).

Places of Birth

1   Chris Smith
2   G. O. Allen
3   Tony and Ian Greig
4   Robin Jackman
5   Ted Dexter

6 D. B. Carr
7 Roland Butcher
8 Bob Woolmer
9 Paul Parker
10 F. R. Brown

Good at Games

1 David Acfield (Essex).

2 Arthur Milton (Gloucs).

3 Martin Donnelly; he played against Ireland.

4 Brian Davison (Leics); he represented Rhodesia at hockey.

5 Andrew Ducat (Surrey and England).

6 A. H. Hornby (Lancs). He captained England at cricket twice, in 1882 and 1884, and at rugby once (1882).
7 J. W. H. T. ('Johnny Won't Hit Today') Douglas (Essex and England).

8 Huddersfield Town.

9 New Zealand full back and pace bowler, Bruce McKechnie. The All Blacks won 13–12.

10 W. G. Grace, who captained England in the first international bowls match in 1903.

11 All these former Surrey cricketers have played in goal for the Corinthian-Casuals football club, whose home ground used to be The Oval.

12 A. H. Pawson.

One-Day Internationals

1 Brian Close.

2 Keith Wadsworth (104).

3   Mike Hendrick (5–31 v Australia, 1980).

4   Dennis Amiss (103 v Australia, 1972; 100 v New Zealand, 1973).

5   Richard Collinge (5–23 v India, 1976).

6   Derek Randall (1 for 2).

7   Gary Sobers.

8   Sarfraz Nawaz (v West Indies).

9   Bruce Laird (117 not out v Pakistan).

10   Barry Wood.

11   Six years.

12   John Bracewell.

Mixed Cricket Bag (2)

1   Eight.

2   The Australian Aboriginals of 1868, the first overseas side to tour England.

3   Maurice Turnbull, 1930 (v New Zealand).

4   Clive Rice.

5   A. E. Relf; he scored 157 and took eight wickets.

6   Damien D'Oliveira (Worcs) and Derek Aslett (Kent).

7   Gary Sobers; he achieved the feat twice.

8   Chris and Alan Old, both playing for England.

9   1956 (v Australia). His first Test before he was ordained was in 1950 (v West Indies).

10   Nottinghamshire (Mike), Surrey (Derek).

11   (a) Mike Gatting (b) Martin Crowe.

12   A. J. Raffles, E. W. Hornung's cricket-playing 'amateur cracksman'.

Hundreds and Hundreds

1   Don Bradman, Glenn Turner, Zaheer Abbas.

2   Arthur Fagg, for Kent v Essex, 1938 (244 and 202 not out).

3   Keith Fletcher, 7hr 38min (England v Pakistan).

4   Robin Hobbs (Essex) in 44min.

5   Alan Melville (v England); the first in 1939, the other three in 1947.

6   C. B. Fry (1901), Mike Procter (1970–1).

7   Graeme Fowler (for Lancs v Warks).

8   98.

9   In batting order: Colin McDonald (127), Neil Harvey (204), Keith Miller (109), Ron Archer (128), Richie Benaud (121).

10   C. P. Mead (Hants).

11   Walter Hammond's.

12   Martin Donnelly (for Oxford 1946, the Gentlemen 1947, New Zealand 1949).

Captains

1   Kim Barnett (Derbys), 23.

2   Ian Craig (v S Africa 1957–8).

3   Cyril Washbrook (1954), Maurice Tremlett (1956), Reg Perks (1955).

4   P. L. van der Merwe.

5   Tom Graveney and Barry Jarman, substituting for Colin Cowdrey and Bill Lawry.

6   Greg Chappell (v West Indies).

7   F. C. M. 'Gerry' Alexander.

8   Hants and Notts.

9   Mark Burgess.

10   Four (3 outright, 1 shared).

11   (a) R. K. Nunes. (b) C. K. Nayudu. (c) B. Warnapura.

12   A. J. Holmes (Sussex).

13   Pakistan v England 1972–3, Majid Khan and A. R. Lewis.

14   M. P. Bowden (Surrey and Transvaal); he captained England once, in the 2nd Test v S Africa in 1889.

15   J. W. H. T. Douglas, while trying to save his father after a collision in the Kattegat in 1930.

16   Abdul Hafeez.

17   R. W. Barber (Lancs), M. C. Cowdrey (Kent), E. R. Dexter (Sussex), M. J. K. Smith (Warks), R. Subba Row (Northants).

18   Hugh Morris (Glam).

19   A. O. Jones (Notts).

20   A. C. MacLaren (108 for Lancs v Sussex, 1890; 200 not out for MCC v New Zealand XI, 1923).

21   In the 4th Test against Australia in 1926 after the appointed captain, A. W. Carr, had retired from the match on the second day with tonsilitis.

22   Keith Carmody, who also introduced the umbrella field for fast bowlers that bears his name.

23   G. R. Viswanath.

24   Tony Greig.

questions on p 22

Badge Spotting

1   Derbys, Hants, Northants.

2   Seaxes.

3   A ragged staff.

4   Glamorgan's daffodil.

5   Martlets; six.

6   Three pears.

7   Blue, gold, brown, silver, green and red.

8   Invicta.

9   The Wessex Wyvern (Somerset).

10   Gold.

11   Ten (two large, eight small).

12   A lion is holding a sword.

Anagrams

1   Keith Miller.

2   Gary Sobers.

3   Godfrey Evans.

4   Lance Cairns.

5   Mohsin Khan.

6   Trevor Bailey.

The Doc and the Don

1 His red and yellow MCC cap.

2 (a).

3 40.

4 Alfred Shaw (Notts), 20 times.

5 While fielding on the boundary, Oxford Blue A. C. M. Croome pierced his throat on a sharp railing. Grace held the gaping wound together for over half an hour to stop the flow of blood, until more sophisticated help arrived.

6 £3000.

7 Cootamundra, NSW.

8 Six.

9 Deputising as wicket-keeper, he pulled off a stumping.

10 None; he played in Tests against South Africa, West Indies and India, but only at home.

11 Seven.

12 Peritonitis following an operation to remove his appendix.

Mixed Cricket Bag (3)

1 Greg Matthews (Australia).

2 George Hirst and Wilfred Rhodes.

3 John Shepherd. He went there with Derrick Robins' side in 1973.

4 Barbados, Leeward Islands, Trinidad, Windward Islands.

5   Karnataka. Their opponents, Delhi, replied with 706 for 8. The match was drawn but Delhi were declared winners of the trophy by virtue of their first-innings lead.

6   Essex, Kent, Essex, Somerset, Surrey, Sussex, Somerset, Derbys and Worcs, Sussex.

7   W. G. Grace was born (18 July).

8   Betty Wilson for Australia v England, 1958. (Her contribution to the match also included the first hat-trick in women's Test cricket.) The first man to achieve this double was Australia's Alan Davidson (v West Indies) in 1960.

9   He broke his toe in the nets.

10   Clifford McWatt (3rd Test v England).

11   Quarndon (Derbys).

12   Ten: bowled; lbw; caught; stumped; run out; hit the ball twice; hit wicket; handled the ball; obstructing the field; timed out.

Record Holders

1   Richie Benaud (2201 runs, 248 wickets).

2   Godfrey Evans; for England v Australia at Adelaide in 1947 (his final score was 10 not out).

3   W. H. Ashdown (Kent). He made his first-class debut for G. Weigall's XI v Oxford University in June 1914 when he was 15, and last played for Maurice Leyland's XI at the Harrogate Festival in 1947.

4   Lance Gibbs.

5   Clyde Walcott; for West Indies v Australia, 1954–5.

6   Derek Underwood (Kent) at the age of 18.

7   Bert Sutcliffe and Don Taylor; for Auckland v Canterbury, 1948–9 (220 and 286).

8 Gary Sobers (8032 runs, 235 wickets, 109 catches).

9 John Reid, in scoring 296 for Wellington v Northern Districts, 1962–3.

10 Derek Shackleton (Hants), 1949–68.

11 Brian Close (Yorks), 1949. He was 18.

12 B. S. Chandrasekhar.

Tests (2)

1 James Lillywhite (Sussex) who captained England in the first two Tests, 1876–7.

2 Seven: R. Willis; F. Trueman; D. Underwood; B. Statham; I. Botham; A. Bedser; J. Snow.

3 Joe Solomon.

4 J. Hampshire; 107 v West Indies, 1969.

5 Tom Veivers (in all he bowled 95.1 overs in England's first innings, taking 3–155).

6 28 years (1973–4).

7 Bill Alley.

8 Warren Bardsley.

9 He had severe toothache.

10 K. S. Ranjitsinhji (154 not out at Old Trafford, 1896).

11 Andrew Hilditch. He had picked up the ball after it had been fielded to hand it to the bowler Sarfraz Nawaz, who successfully appealed.

12 Len Hutton (165 not out) and Denis Compton (10 not out) – 3rd Test v West Indies at The Oval, August 1939.

Limited Overs

1 Norman Gifford (Worcs).

2 (a) Geoffrey Boycott (146); (b) Ray Illingworth (5–29). Both for Yorks v Surrey, 1965.

3 Peter Marner, 121 for Lancs v Leics, 1963.

4 Hants.

5 Geoff Miller and Colin Tunnicliffe.

6 541.

7 Essex. Warwickshire replied with 301 for 6 in 39.3 overs.

8 Gordon Greenidge (Hants), 17 sixes.

9 Yorkshire (to Leics).

10 Ken Higgs, for Leics v Surrey.

11 Lancs 1969–70.

12 Vic Marks (Somerset).

13 Mike Llewellyn (Glam) was the batsman; John Emburey (Middx) the bowler. It was in 1977 and Middx won.

14 Durham beat Yorks in 1973.

15 Jack Simmons.

16 Graham Gooch's (for Essex v Sussex).

17 Transvaal.

18 Jim Cumbes – Lancs, Surrey, Worcs, Warks.

19 David Larter (v Sussex).

20 Keith Boyce, 8–26 for Essex v Lancs, 1971.

21 New Zealand.

22 David Bairstow. His partner was Mark Johnson, and Yorks won by one wicket.

23 Brian Langford (v Essex).

24 Northants – the Gillette Cup.

Around the Grounds

1   (a) Dunedin, New Zealand (b) Bridgetown, Barbados
(c) Port Elizabeth, S Africa (d) Delhi, India (e) St John's,
Antigua.

2   Trent Bridge.

3   Fiji (Churchill Park is in Lautoka).

4   Aylestone Road.

5   130,000.

6   Bramall Lane, Sheffield.

7   Swansea. (These are the opening lines of John Arlott's
poem *Cricket at Swansea*.)

8   Prince's Ground, Chelsea (1872–6).

9   Saravanamuttu Stadium, Colombo.

10   Brentwood.

11   McLean Park, Napier.

12   Woolloongabba, Brisbane.

Cricketing Dates

1   1787.

2   1969.

3   1962.

4   1948 (v Australia).

5   1930 (21 February: 4th Test New Zealand v England;
3rd Test West Indies v England. The only occasion that any
country has played in two official Test series at the same
time.)

6   1864.

7   1981 (v Australia at Trent Bridge).

8   1899 (1st Test v Australia).

9   1928, 1930, 1932, 1954.

10   1864.

11   1968.

12   1814.

Cricketing Nobs

1   Hon Charles Lyttelton (later Viscount Cobham), Worcs.

2   Hon (later Lord) Lionel Tennyson, Hants and England, grandson of the poet Alfred Tennyson.

3   Learie Constantine.

4   Hon Tim Lamb, Northants.

5   Sir C. Aubrey Smith, who captained England in what was both his and S Africa's first Test match in 1889. It was his only Test appearance, and he went on to greater fame as a Hollywood film actor.

6   Sir John Berry Hobbs.

7   Hon Ivo Bligh (later Earl of Darnley). As captain of the victorious England side to Australia in 1882–3, he was presented by some Australian ladies with the ashes of a bail or stump sealed in an urn – a sequel to the famous mock obituary notice that had appeared in *The Sporting Times* after Australia's earlier triumph in England. On Bligh's death in 1927, The Ashes were passed on to the MCC.

8   Prince K. S. Duleepsinhji, Sussex and England.

9   Rt Hon Sir F. S. Jackson (Yorks). England won the five-match series in 1905 two-nil. Jackson scored 492 runs (70.28) and took 13 wickets (15.46).

10   'Lord Beginner' (Egbert Moore); West Indies won the
2nd Test at Lord's in 1950 by 326 runs.

11   Sir Timothy O'Brien (Middx and Ireland), who played
five times for England and captained them once – in S
Africa in 1896 when Lord Hawke was unfit.

12   Sir Gajapatairaj Vijaya Ananda, The Maharajkumar
of Vizianagram, understandably known as 'Vizzy'.

Mixed Cricket Bag (4)

1   Clive Radley (Middx).

2   He was an American. John Barton King of the touring
Gentlemen of Philadelphia took 87 wickets in the season at
11.01 runs each.

3   John Hampshire and Tony Nicolson.

4   The ukelele.

5   Trinidad & Tobago.

6   The Jordan Rosebowl.

7   R. Abel, T. Hayward, G. Lohmann, T. Richardson (all
Surrey) and G. Gunn (Notts). The asking price per man was
£20. In the event, Abel, Hayward and Gunn played and, it
is said, were eventually paid their £20, though it was never
officially recorded.

8   They were the first touring party to arrive in England by
plane.

9   Five (1900–4).

10   F. R. Spofforth, for Australia v England at Melbourne
in 1879. He took 13–110 in the match.

11   John Wright.

12   (b) on horseback.

ANSWERS questions on pp 33–40

Picture Questions

1 (a) Five Western Australians selected to tour England in 1972. Watching Dennis Lillee give blood are (*from left*) Ross Edwards, Graeme Watson, Rodney Marsh and Bob Massie.

(b) The angelic features of choirboy Jim Laker in 1929.

(c) Alan Ward (Derbys) training with the Chesterfield Football Club prior to joining the MCC touring party to Australia in 1970.

2 (a) Frank Hayes is the fieldsman, Gary Gilmour the batsman. The others are (*clockwise from left*): batsman Doug Walters, Tony Greig, Barry Wood, Keith Fletcher, Alan Knott, John Snow, Peter Lever, Mike Denness. England v Australia, Prudential World Cup Semi-Final, 1975.

(b) Madan Lal bowled by Mike Hendrick, England v India at Old Trafford, 1974. The ball dipped in very late to hit the inside of the off stump; then flicked the middle stump, pushing it back an inch or two, before striking the leg stump.

3 (a) Geoffrey Boycott, batting for England v West Indies at Port-of-Spain in 1968. Appealing are Deryck Murray and Lance Gibbs. Boycott was given out lbw to David Holford for 68.

(b) Richie Benaud in full swing for The Australians v Worcestershire 1953. Hugo Yarnold is the wicket-keeper, Laddie Outschoorn is at slip.

4 (a) Former Yorks captain W. H. 'Billy' Sutcliffe, son of Herbert.

(b) Indian Test batsman Ashok Mankad, son of 'Vinoo'.

5 Two great fast bowlers:

(a) Brian Statham (Lancs and England).

(b) Fazal Mahmood (Northern India, Punjab and Pakistan).

6 (a) Dick Howorth (Worcs and England).
(b) Sony Ramadhin (Trinidad, Lancs and West Indies).
(c) 'Sam' Cook (Gloucs and England).

7 (a) Brendon Bracewell (Central Districts and New Zealand).

(b) Jeff Hammond (S Australia and Australia).

(c) Alan Connolly (Victoria, Middx and Australia).

8 (a) Collis King, who had just been dismissed after a magnificent 86 for West Indies v England in the 1979 Prudential World Cup Final. Richards himself went on to score 138 not out.

(b) Graham Stevenson, on reaching his century while batting at No 11 for Yorks v Warks in 1982. Boycott and Stevenson put on 149 for the last wicket (Boycott 79, Stevenson 115 not out).

Bowlers

1 Phil Edmonds (Middx) and Derek Underwood (Kent).

2 E. L. McCormick.

3 For not announcing that he was about to bowl underarm.

4 Charles Palmer (Leics). He finished with 8 for 7.

5 Clarrie Grimmett, who played for Australia though he was New Zealand born. He took 216 Test wickets in all.

6 Venkataraghavan, the Indian off-spinner.

7 N. I. Thomson (Sussex), who took 10–49 v Warks in 1964.

8 Fazal Mahmood. His final tally was 139.

9 Pat Pocock (Surrey) v Sussex in a County Championship match. He finished with 7–67.

10 M. R. Dilley (v Notts and Sussex).

11 Nasim-ul-Ghani. Pakistan won the match by an innings and 1 run.

12 Alan Ward (Derbys).

13   Malcolm Marshall (Hants), 134. Second highest was Nick Cook with 90.

14   Len Durtanovich (his family is Yugoslavian).

15   Don Shepherd (Glam).

16   A. E. Trott's (154 wickets in 1900).

17   G. Geary and H. A. Smith. They dismissed Worcs in their 2nd innings for 77, then Gloucs for 72 (only one innings was played), followed by Northants for 85 and 79.

18   Australian Jack Iverson, who puzzled many batsmen with his spin during his short first-class career (1949–53). He developed his technique by flicking a ping-pong ball against a post.

19   Roley Jenkins (Worcs).

20   Atholl McKinnon.

21   He was knocked down by a passing vehicle, while trying to stop traffic at the scene of an accident in which his own car had been involved. He was 45.

22   Somerset. He played for them in 1905.

23   Jeff Jones (Glam) with 15 wickets (35.53).

24   Eddie Gilbert (Queensland) and Tim Wall (S Australia).

Partners

1   Bob Barber (Lancs/Warks).

2   Cliff Gladwin (Derbys).

3   'Vinoo' Mankad (231) and Pankaj Roy (173) for India v New Zealand at Madras. The previous record was 359, scored by Len Hutton (158) and Cyril Washbrook (195) against S Africa at Jo'burg in 1948.

4 Tom Goddard and Cecil ('Sam') Cook of Gloucs. Goddard played in eight Tests, Cook in one.

5 Clive Lloyd and David Lloyd; v Gloucs.

6 G. A. Faulkner, R. O. Schwarz, G. C. White, A. E. E. Vogler.

7 12 years (Hobbs was 41, Sutcliffe 29).

8 95 – a Test record for individual catches off one bowler.

9 Graham Roope. Boycott's came in the 4th Test against Australia at Headingley; Edrich's in a County Championship match for Surrey against Derbys.

10 K. Farnes (Essex) and C. I. J. Smith (Middx), England's opening bowlers and makeshift opening batsmen in the 2nd innings.

11 D. B. Vengsarkar (ret'd hurt 71), G. R. Viswanath (222), Yashpal Sharma (140).

12 (a) Cannings (Hants)   (e) Brown (Middx)
    (b) Harris (Notts)   (f) Jepson (Notts)
    (c) Coldwell (Worcs)   (g) Place (Lancs)
    (d) Manning (Northants) (h) Knott (Kent).

Initial Questions

1 Keith William Robert FLETCHER.

2 Robert George Dylan WILLIS.

3 Isaac Vivian Alexander RICHARDS.

4 Douglas Vivian Parson WRIGHT.

5 Leslie Ethelbert George AMES.

6 Anderson Montgomery Everton ROBERTS.

7 Roger David Verdon KNIGHT.

8 Graham Anthony Richard LOCK.

9   Robert Walter Vivian ROBINS.

10   George Hubert Graham DOGGART.

11   Eldine Ashworth Elderfield BAPTISTE.

12   Paul William Giles PARKER.

13   Alan Philip Eric KNOTT.

14   Arthur Percy Frank CHAPMAN.

15   Nicholas Edward Julian POCOCK.

16   John Henry Bickford WAITE.

17   John Robert Troutbeck BARCLAY.

18   George Oswald Browning ('Gubby') ALLEN.

19   Nigel Francis Mark POPPLEWELL.

20   Graham Richard James ROOPE.

Anagrams

1   Richard Hadlee.

2   Martin Crowe.

3   Bob Willis.

4   Hugh Tayfield.

5   Everton Weekes.

6   Eric Bedser; Alec Bedser.

Who's Who

1   Ted Dexter (the winning candidate was James Callaghan).

2   Alfred Mynn (Kent), George Parr (Notts).

3   Graham Roope.

4   Alfred Shaw was the 'bowler', Arthur Shrewsbury the 'batsman'. Both played for Notts and England.

5   Sir Pelham Warner.

6   Keith Ross Miller (the aviators were Keith Smith and Ross Smith).

7   John Arlott.

8   Enid Bakewell, in the 1970 edition.

9   Winston Churchill.

10   Fred Trueman.

11   Gilbert Jessop of Gloucs and England. He was trapped in a heat-treatment box while seeking a cure for lumbago in 1916. As a result his heart was seriously damaged, thus ending his career at the age of 42.

12   The nineteenth-century cricketer Nicholas Wanostrocht, better known as 'N. Felix'.

13   Rupert Howard.

14   Brian Close.

15   Frederick Louis, Prince of Wales, son of George II. He died in 1751 from an injury caused by a cricket ball, thus depriving England of its first King Frederick.

16   Former Pakistan Test opener, Aftab Gul.

17   Former Lancs and England wicket-keeper George Duckworth, who was baggage-master for a number of touring teams after the war.

18   The Duke of Wellington.

19   Jack Fingleton.

20   Keith Andrew.

21   Bobby Peel in 1897. The county was Yorks and the captain Lord Hawke.

22   West Indian fast bowler Roy Gilchrist from the 1958–9 tour of India and Pakistan.

23   Geoffrey Boycott.

24   Dwight D. Eisenhower, who attended the fourth day of the 3rd Test between Pakistan and Australia at Karachi in 1959.

Weights and Measures

1   $5\frac{1}{2}$–$5\frac{3}{4}$oz (155.9g–163g).

2   The 10.00am start.

3   Yorks (19.77), Derbys (18.24).

4   67yd 6in. R. D. Burrows was the bowler, for Worcs v Lancs, 1911.

5   £128,000.

6   13ft 3in.

7   The Oval, 6 acres.

8   6ft 6in.

9   1939.

10   5ft (1.52m) 'on either side of a line joining the centre of the middle stumps of the wickets'.

11   Kent (58.09), Glam (45.28).

12   Barry Richards – he earned $1538.

Overseas Players in England

1   Northants, Notts, Somerset, Sussex, Somerset.

2   Alf Gover's Cricket School.

3   Tom Pritchard, Warks.

4   Danny *Livingstone* (Hants), Jock *Livingston* (Northants).

5   Sylvester Clarke (Surrey).

6   Mike Whitney, the Australian pace bowler and on-the-spot replacement for the injured Hogg and Lawson. He was summoned from relative obscurity after only six first-class matches to play in the 5th and 6th Tests against England.

7   Lee Irvine (1968).

8   Frank Tarrant; he played for Middx from 1904–14.

9   Gamini Goonesena, later of Notts and Ceylon.

10   J. J. Ferris (Gloucs), W. E. Midwinter (Gloucs), W. L. Murdoch (Sussex), A. E. Trott (Middx), S. M. J. Woods (Somerset).

11   'A' is Dilip Doshi, 'B' is Alvin Kallicharran. They were both playing for Warks.

12   Colin McCool (father) played for the county from 1956–60; Russell McCool (son) made his debut in 1982.

World Cup

1   Sunil Gavaskar (v England).

2   Sri Lanka and East Africa.

3   Gary Gilmour (5–48 v West Indies).

4   Dennis Amiss (137 v India) and Keith Fletcher (131 v New Zealand); Glenn Turner (171 not out v E Africa; 114 not out v India).

5   Alan Turner, 101 for Australia v Sri Lanka, 1975.

6   Bermuda, Denmark, Canada, Sri Lanka – the last two went through to the World Cup.

7   Gibraltar.

8   With a six off Mike Hendrick.

9   Mike Brearley (64).

10   Four.

11   Graham Gooch (v Australia and New Zealand).

12   Winston Davis, 7–51 for West Indies v Australia, 1983.

13   Madan Lal (caught Kapil Dev for 33).

14   100 (6 sixes, 16 fours).

15   Abdul Qadir (v New Zealand and Sri Lanka).

16   Duncan Fletcher (v Australia, 1983).

17   Sri Lanka; L. Mendis and S. Wettimuny.

18   Derek Pringle's (his father Donald played for E Africa).

19   Five.

20   Canada.

21   Sri Lanka (288 for 9 in reply to Pakistan's 338 for 5).

22   Bob Willis – for his captaincy (England won by 9 wickets).

23   £4000.

24   Seven (Lloyd, Greenidge, Haynes, Richards, Roberts, Garner, Holding).

Accidents will Happen

1   Peter Pollock, Neil Adcock, Charlie Griffith, Graham McKenzie, Tony Greig.

2   Wes Hall was the bowler, Colin Cowdrey's the arm.

3   A. H. Bakewell, 1936; Colin Milburn, 1969.

4   Australian batsman Rick Darling.

5   Don Bradman.

6   England physiotherapist Bernard Thomas; Peter Lever was the bowler.

7   Len Hutton, Fred Titmus, Nawab of Pataudi (Jnr).

8   Geoff Howarth, Jeff Crowe.

9   Dick Pollard (he was batting at the time and hit Barnes, who was fielding at shortleg, in the ribs with a full-blooded stroke).

10   Bob Willis was the bowler, Rick McCosker's the jaw.

11   Gary Sobers.

12   LBW.

Tests (3)

1   Sarfraz Nawaz, for Pakistan v Australia at Melbourne. He finished with 9–86 and Pakistan won by 71 runs.

2   Tony Greig; 148 and 6–164 v West Indies at Bridgetown, 1974.

3   Hit wicket.

4   R. G. Nadkarni (32–27–5–0). He bowled 21 consecutive maidens, a record for all first-class cricket.

5   Shoaib Mohammad (son of Hanif). Zaheer had a groin injury.

6   G. E. Gomez, a last-minute replacement as umpire, was a West Indian Test selector at the time.

7   Four: C. Bannerman, T. Kendall, W. Midwinter, N. Thompson.

8   Philip Sharpe (Yorks, later Derbys).

9   Ken Cranston (Lancs). His final figures were 4–12 and England won by 10 wickets.

10   A wicket with their first ball in Test cricket.

11   Sandeep Patil of India was the batsman; Bob Willis the bowler. There was one no-ball in the over.

12   Allan Watkins' (Glam).

Behind the Stumps

1   Godfrey Evans (his final total was 1060).

2   30.

3   Leslie Ames; 120 at Lord's, 1934.

4   David East (Essex), 68.

5   Rodney Marsh, 1981.

6   D. D. Hindlekar.

7   None. He played in four but only as a batsman (v India 1976–7).

8   Don Tallon 1938–9, Brian Taber 1968–9.

9   Hugo Yarnold, for Worcs v Scotland, 1951. He stumped six and caught one.

10   Denis Lindsay, for S Africa v Australia, 1966. He scored 182 and caught six in Australia's 1st innings.

11   E. C. Petrie.

12   W. L. Murdoch, v S Africa 1892. He was deputising for H. Wood in the 2nd innings.

13   H. 'Sammy' Carter.

14   Alan Knott.

15   John Waite, for S Africa v New Zealand 1961–2. Marsh established a new record of 28 dismissals, v England 1982–3.

16   The 47-year-old Frank Woolley, deputising for the lumbago stricken Leslie Ames. He conceded a record total of 37 byes out of a score of 327; but he did take one catch.

17   Imtiaz Ahmed.

18   West Indian S. C. Guillen, playing for New Zealand. Guillen had previously played in five Tests for West Indies and was to play in three for his new country.

19   Steve Rixon.

20   J. T. Murray (Middx), 1957 – 1025 runs, 104 dismissals.

21   David East (Essex), Geoff Humpage (Warks), Trevor Gard (Somerset).

22   Rohan Kanhai. F. C. M. Alexander took over for the 4th and 5th Tests, though Kanhai retained his place in the side as a batsman.

23   Bert Oldfield (Australia), 52 in 54 Tests.

24   They both constitute a religious minority in their national side. In 1984 Anil Dalpat became the first Hindu to play for the predominantly Muslim Pakistan; and Syed Kirmani is one of the very few Muslims to have played for the mainly Hindu Indian team.

Mixed Cricket Bag (5)

1   Peter Toohey (122).

2   Scotland.

3   A market garden.

4   Rachel Heyhoe-Flint, v Australia at The Oval, 1963.

5   E. R. Dexter (quoted in his autobiography *Ted Dexter Declares*).

6   Rhyming slang: bunsen burner/raging turner. A pitch taking a lot of spin.

7   G. H. Simpson-Hayward (Worcs). He played for England in just five Tests, v S Africa in 1909–10, taking 23 wickets in the series.

8   Norman Cowans.

9   Paris.

10   Bishan Bedi; he made his debut for Northern Punjab in 1961–2.

11   Wes Hall's, for West Indies v Pakistan at Lahore in 1959.

12   (a) a 45lb salmon.

Super Quiz Rules

PRIZES: 1st prize: One week self catering for two in Greece, courtesy of Olympic Holidays.
Prizes 2–10: Double tickets to England v Australia Test Match, Lords 1985.
Prizes 11–40: Copy of *The Lord's Taverners 50 Greatest* book.

1 All correct entries will be put into a hat, and the first 50 entries drawn out will receive the above prizes, in order. Contest and book sales commence 27 September 1984.

2 The book must be purchased to participate in the contest. An original entry form is included in all books. Only original entry forms will be accepted.

3 A ballpoint pen must be used to complete the entry form. The completed entry form should be sent to The Lord's Taverners Super Quiz, David & Charles Ltd, Brunel House, Forde Road, Newton Abbot, Devon TQ12 1PU.

4 Any entrants under 18 years of age should indicate their age on the entry form and their parent's or guardian's permission to enter.

5 All entries are the property of David & Charles Ltd and none will be returned.

6 No correspondence will be entered into regarding the competition.

7 All entries must be received at the above address no later than 15 February 1985. Any entries arriving after that date will not be accepted. The publishers accept no responsibility for lost or damaged entry forms.

8 Winners will be notified by post.

9 The judges' decision is final.

10 All employees of David & Charles and their families and anyone else connected with the publication of *The Lord's Taverners Cricket Quiz Book* are ineligible for the competition.

11 The competition is only open to residents of the United Kingdom and the Republic of Ireland.

Super Quiz
Entry Form

THE LORD'S TAVERNERS SUPER QUIZ

Print your name and address in the spaces provided and
send the completed answer sheet to:

David & Charles (Lord's Taverners Super Quiz)
Brunel House
Forde Road
Newton Abbot
Devon TQ12 1PU

Name ....

Address ....

....

....

....

Telephone (day)................. (evening) ....

Age (if under 18) ....

I hereby give permission for ....

.... to enter The Lord's Taverners Super Quiz

....(parent/guardian).

I hereby agree to abide by the rules of the competition.

Signed ....

Date ....

Closing date for entries 15 February 1985

Super Quiz

Write correct answer in space provided.

1   What cut short John Edrich's appearance in the 3rd Test against New Zealand at Auckland in 1966?

....

2   What was the name of the boys' club in Cambridge that had the young Jack Hobbs as a founder member?

....

3   Who was the first batsman to score 2000 runs in a season for Somerset?

....

4   Which one-time England cricketer wrote a book about his POW exploits in the First World War, entitled *The Escaping Club*?

....

5   Which England soccer international in 1947 took a wicket with his first ball in first-class cricket, in what was his first and last county match, and for whom was he playing?

....

6   Which famous English writer who died in 1946 was the son of a professional cricketer?

....

7   Who was the first representative of Western Australia to win a Test cap for his country?

....

8   Which former Warwickshire cricketer lent his name to one of the great comic characters of modern English fiction?

....

9   Whose supporters stopped play at Headingley in the 3rd Test between England and Australia in 1975?

....

10   Who was the former Surrey and England cricketer Andrew Ducat playing for when he dropped dead at the wicket at Lord's in 1942?

....

11   Which county turned down Wilfred Rhodes when he applied to join it in 1897?

....

12   Who were the victorious opponents of Dingley Dell?

....

13   What held up play in the County Championship match between Gloucestershire and Derbyshire at Gloucester in 1957:
a) a hedgehog on the field   b) an eclipse of the sun or c) a helicopter landing?

....

14   Who in 1981 dismissed Geoffrey Boycott with his first delivery in first-class cricket?

....

15   Which Test cricketer's bowling arm was withered by polio when he was five years old?

....

16   When was the Centenary of Tom Brown's match: MCC v Rugby School?

....

17   Who was the only Yorkshireman to captain England between F. S. Jackson in 1905 and Norman Yardley in 1947?

....

18   Who was Peter May playing for when he made his first-class debut?

....

19   Which former West Indian cricketer was appointed Guyana's Junior Minister of Sport in December 1980?

....

20   Which Test ground is overlooked by the Port Hills?

....

21   Who 'ghosted' John Nyren's book, *The Cricketers of my Time*?

....

22   Whose ashes were discovered in a cardboard box in a Sydney funeral parlour in 1972, 28 years after his death?

....

23   Who was the first professional cricketer to be elected an England Test Selector?

....

24   What were the real names of the famous cricketing cartoonists 'Ape' and 'Spy'?

....

25   Which England wicket-keeper took 4—19 in a Test against Australia?

....

26   Where and in what year was the first Test match to be televised in England?

....

27   Who was 'The Battersea Bradman'?

....

28   In the name of which American writer of thrillers will you find a pair of fast bowlers?

....

29   Which post-war England cricket captain was a hockey international goalkeeper?

....

30   Who kept wicket for the Australian Services side in England in 1945?

....

31   Which former Lancashire and England batsman has on his tombstone the inscription 'Bowled at Last'?

....

32   Who returned to English first-class cricket in 1948 after an absence of 11 years and scored three centuries in his first four matches?

....

33   Who was the West Indian fast bowler hanged in 1955 for the murder of his wife?

....

34   During the MCC v Cambridge University match at Lord's in 1936 a sparrow was killed by a ball bowled by Jahangir Khan. Who was the batsman who managed to play the ball as the bird hit the stumps?

....